GW00471826

QUEEN OWL WINGS

A collection of poems by

JEANNETTE ENCINIAS

Copyright © 2021 by Jeannette Encinias

All rights reserved. No part of this book may be reproduced or used in any manner without written permission of the copyright owner except for the use of quotations in a book review. For more information, address: billelliot@elliot.com

FIRST EDITION

Interior Book Design & Typesetting by Ines Monnet
Cover Design by Victoria O'May

www.jeannetteencinias.com

ISBN: 978-0-578-84541-8

For my parents, Anne and Albert Encinias
Thank you for nurturing my poet's heart.

July 2023.

Darling Mollie ♥

*I feel every word in
this book could have
been written by you.*

*Thank you for being my
little light next door*

*with much love
and rose petal tea*

Vikki xxx

Contents

Nourished

I worry seriously
about only a handful of things.
Eyes to the ground
furrowed brow
beating heart
sleep.

Then I remember
that I am here right now.
Here—
with good work and a big, bright love.
With a dog who just had a bath
after running in the mud.
With a mother who gardens and does yoga
and a father who makes rosaries and reads books.
And my brother, my friend, with a sweet baby daughter.

And I have my legs
and they walk for miles when I worry.
And I have my soul
and it is vast and kinder
than this wild world.
And I have books
with their strong spines and medicine.

And music, all the music
and there is the mailman
who delivers mail almost every single day
bless him.

And the market with wine and radishes.
And the flowers falling through my hands
trusting me to make bouquets.
And there is the green earth and the tall mountain
the water birds, seedlings, snowfall, the sound of rain,
sun finally
spring!

The bed and the water.
The paper and the pens.
The bathtub and the salt.
And the food he made me
and the letter she sent me
and Spain, San Francisco,
your bedroom, this kitchen.

It's all been so much beauty among
the worry.
And I have kept nourished
and alive
this way.

Beneath The Sweater And The Skin

How many years of beauty do I have left?
she asks me.
How many more do you want?
Here. Here is 34. Here is 50.

When you are 80 years old
and your beauty rises in ways
your cells cannot even imagine now
and your wild bones grow luminous and
ripe, having carried the weight
of a passionate life.

When your hair is aflame
with winter
and you have decades of
learning and leaving and loving
sewn into
the corners of your eyes
and your children come home
to find their own history
in your face.

When you know what it feels like to fail
ferociously
and have gained the
capacity
to rise and rise and rise again.

When you can make your tea
on a quiet and ridiculously lonely afternoon
and still have a song in your heart,
Queen owl wings beating
beneath the cotton of your sweater.

Because your beauty began there
beneath the sweater and the skin,
remember?

This is when I will take you
into my arms and coo
YOU BRAVE AND GLORIOUS THING
you've come so far.
I see you.
Your beauty is breathtaking.

Rise

I was a lantern then.
Barely any light at all.
Not yet knowing
how to use my lungs,
afraid of my own fire.

Simmer down,
he said.
Until
eventually
I was just smoke
moving up
past windows
above rooftops
learning the curve
of the moon
the constitution
of trees
in the quietest
hours of night
these things showed me
how to live.

Until one morning
brimming with sky
and stars

I came back
to my lantern life
and my light was so large
it would not fit.

My fire so bright
it burned our whole house
down.

Simmer down!
Simmer down!
he cried.

I cannot.
I never will
said my
eyes.

Until his words
were only ashes
swept clean
into a small corner
not fit for fire.

Love

My saving grace.
My gentle phenomenon.
I see you in the sunlit song of water.
I whisper the weather to the trees
so they know to hang over you
when storm pulls in.

You Will Be Changed

You will be changed—
by the heartbreak
by the joy
by the failure
by the beauty
by the art
by the love.

You will be changed—
by the work
by the aging
by the sky
by the music
by the sorrow
by the death
by the birth.

And then what will happen
is that you will meet yourself again, new.

Oh, hello, it's you.
How you've grown!

Other people may not recognize you.
They may say you've changed.

You will lift your chin.
You will open your eyes.
You will surely agree.

But before all this
there is the in-between.

The seemingly endless
unraveling.
The tender fledgling.
The, I don't know what on earth is happening!

It will be uncomfortable.
It will be messy.
Let it be.

Dirt, dark and fertile, stirring.
Days, long and lonely, leveling.

When you're changing
it may feel like you're breaking.
Or, like you're out to sea alone
with no boat,
flailing.

Will you drown?
Will you learn to swim?
No one can really say
except for you.

You.

You have permission
to change
from who you've been
to who you are becoming.
Just as nature does
continuously.

You are not here on earth
to remain the same.
You are an alive and original thing.
Unfurl your wings.
And when the time is right—
fly, fly, fly!

Body

I understand now
how eternal it all is.

How this body
is a beautiful dress
I get to wear
for a few chapters
in time.

And so
I speak to it well.
I make it mine.

Heroine

You don't have to make your bed
and lie in it.
You don't have to toe the line.
No need to explain yourself.
No need to apologize for the 29th time
for nothing.

I want you to know
that we were taught this bullshit.
To please
to be quiet
to stand in line
to be written out
of our own story.

We can unlearn it
and we must,
fast.

Here, I have sharpened these pencils.
Take them and sharpen some more.
Pass them on.
Write a new story.
Begin with yourself
as the heroine.

Morning

I see you in the morning.
Your face still tender from sleep.
Your eyes still a part of
that other inner world
I can never follow you to.

You always wake before I do.
You shuffle to the light
of the kitchen
and scratch your beard.
You have been growing it long
these days
and I have been cutting my hair.

Our bodies touch in small ways
as we begin the day because
we need our own bodies first
to steady ourselves
for the tasks ahead.

Until one of us must leave
the house and then
we circle each other
with strong arms.
Draw nets of protection
around each other's dear souls.

I have tremendous love for you.
I first felt it growing
all along my collarbone
one afternoon
years ago and I was
surprised by how it felt
or that I was given a chance
to feel it.

It was the strangest sensation—
warm, alive, its own force.
Like water rising along my skin.
There was never a fear of drowning
just a strong desire to learn
how to swim.

And I know now that love
is a luxury.
That the country of this love
has changed me.

I was just a foreigner before
never really knowing
how to speak
or how to be understood.

Fumbling with my words
clutching at maps
getting lost.

It was only when
I let all of that go—
the striving
the need to be
held, to be understood
to be half of something
that I became who I am.

And there you were
and here you are.
Preparing the early coffee.
All the morning birds
smiling.

The Mind Is A Maze

The trees are bare
and my mind is a maze.

I circle death
while never leaving
the body.

Death is not frightening.
The stories of the mind are.
I know this and so
I put them to bed
one by one.

It takes all day
and it is so tedious.
And it is good work.

When the darkness comes in hot
and threatens to burn your house down
breathe deep into your chest.

That is where
the water is.

Hammock

She looked at me as if I had
a hammock in my eyes where she
could come lie down and rest.

So I tethered myself between two trees
fashioned the strands of my hair into a book
and my eyes into a bowl of water.

I will stay here 100 summers, I said.
There is no rush with friendship.
There is no hurry with love.

Free

I cut my hair
I bend my back
to ease my spine
to free my neck.

I don't need it—

your approval
your criticism
your praise.

I have shoulders
built from
the soul of
my mother.

I have
sass so strong
handed straight down
from my grandmother.

And my great grandmother
that sweet witch
slapping her knee
spirit howling
blood boiling
perfume whispering—

Pick up the boots, baby.
String on the pearls.

I chop the onion.
I cut the lemon.
I take the dress down.
I wear it.

I move my body out
to talk to the sky
and when the time comes
I will leave it there.

The life I lived
made with sovereignty
and with
love.

Gathering Light For Winter

When you have no words for the wounds.
When your body is as hollowed out and dark
as a jack-o-lantern in November.
When you have lost your north, your south,
your east, and your west
stay still.

Words for the pain are forming
beneath the skin of your patience.
Your body is gathering light for winter.
Your compass is emerging through water.

Sometimes dying is the only way to live again.
It may take all your stories away.
It may hunt and kill your pride
so you are left with nothing
but questions and space
howling into the night, asking
What next? What now? What for?

This is when grace
pours her warm milk
into your wounds
and advises you to rest.
To steal the secrets of sorrow
and learn her heavy song
so that you can become an instrument

of resilience, turning ever forward
with more than you were born with.

For isn't holding hands with sorrow
a bridge?
Dying while you are still alive.
Birthing your next self
and courageously
beginning anew.

Choices

A ship at sea can change her landfall
by a thousand miles
with a mere two degree shift
in her present course.

You can too.

You can pivot.
You can change your direction.
You can love what you really love
and land in a place
that feels more like
home.

Dogs

Our dogs died
last summer.
One in his sleep
the other in my arms.
In quick succession
they were gone.

The summer was hot and
painful.
Beautiful in its own way.

It's cooler now
almost one year later.
We have our heads on straighter
and patched up hearts.
So we go to the dog park
and watch the dogs run.

We sit on the bench
hip to hip.
Our chins propped
in the palms of our hands.

We don't have children
except that we did.
Their eyes were shaped
like almonds and pears.

They howled and hiccupped
in their sleep.
They gave us reason
to walk around the block.
They stole our bed and our hearts.

Look at that one, I say.
He's so fast!
I bet he's very happy.
I mean, look at him!
Yeah, that's a good one.
You can tell, Trev says.
Look how good he is.

Our eyes are dryer now
so we can see their
blooming faces.
Chins lifted up in anticipation.
Tails, an expression of emotion.

My eyes leap from my own face.
My heart ready
to maybe
love again.

But this is just research really.
I am looking for how to use my arms

after Lilly
and that takes time.

Meanwhile, come here.
Sit beside me and
watch the dogs run.
Tell me again
why you love them.
The way they trust.
Their devotion.
Their deep loyalty.
And while we're at it,
let's talk about the chapel of trees.
How they bow and sway.
The way the sky is still there
when we wake up
even though our dogs have died.
The way that flower
has completely seduced
the branch.
Mighty birds
orchestrating the wind.

How love always returns.
How nothing ever really dies.
It's enough to just remember that.
Sometimes that is enough.

Alchemy

When I came to you
I was one way
and now I leave
someone else.

I thought I knew
exactly who I was.

How wrong.
How naive to think
that in your hands
earth would not burn.

Love alchemizes us all.
This is its gift.

And when the fire clears
and smoke makes room for sky.
When my lungs can again remember
what they were
made for
and my chest can finally
take back
the muscle of
my own heart.

Then I will climb
the tallest mountain

and tell every bird
the story of us
so that they may
thread their nests
with sweetness and
with salt.

Joy

It comes when you least expect it.
A moment poured from the sky
just for you.

It will probably land
down the length of your neck
or on your shoulders
and feel warm like the sun.

Your chin will lift
if only for a moment
eyelashes to cheeks
breath calm and rhythmic
in your chest.

No work to do.
Nothing to prove.

Open this moment.
Let it love you.
This joy is for you.

Lonely

The loneliness has always been here
even though I am rarely alone.
It moves along my shoulders and fumbles through my chest.
It settles there.
It scratches at the back of my brain.
A little animal.
Fearful and separate.

It creates castles of loss
and I sometimes wander
those vast halls
though I know the way to the door.

It reminds me of my darkness.
I howl at it.
I rage against it.
Until finally,
I turn my neck toward it
and dip my head.

Come here,
I offer to the loneliness.
Come, tell me what you know.

Don't Abandon Yourself

Not when you're sick.
Now when you're tired.
Not when you've lost
the thread
the thought
or the thing you thought
defined you.

You will die many times
in one life
and create yourself
anew.

This is natural.
This is a gift.
I've died a few times now
here in this world.
The person I was—
gone.

Throw that older skin into the water.
Give it to the sky.
Step into what wants to emerge now.
Nothing can hold you back
when you are willing
to be yourself.

Hot

The anger rises hot like lava
when you least expect it.

Your cool and pretty face
grows horns so sharp
it could implore a man
to impale himself
if he crosses you.

You don't apologize for it.
You are all out of those.

Sorry is a word you learned
to appease a mischief that
wasn't yours.

Instead
you show your neck
raise your chin
arrow your eyes.

You've grown wise
so now you are
seething.
Beside yourself.
Watching the anger move
like a silent film.

You never intended to lose
your voice
or to make it bend
into an octave above
the roots of your throat.

So when the anger comes
it is without restraint
from a thousand
little cuts
that finally formed
a hot pool in the pit
of your eyes.

They had been waiting.
Those eyes.
This mouth.
These fists.

Because you didn't come here to be pretty.
You didn't come here to be nice.
You are not Rapunzel.
You are not soft and malleable like dough.

You come
from a people
who were burned.

Who could not tolerate
eyes full of wolves.
Who would rather die
than lie down.

So when you stand up now
it is with
an entire sea of women
at your back and
by your side.
Their own mischief
unfurling through
your veins.

Simplicity

Life will consistently
humble us until
we are so close
to the ground
that we understand
the startling beauty
of simplicity
and earth.

The Year I Stopped Writing Poetry

If you saw me on the street
you could say I looked confused.
Out of breath and aimless.
You probably thought to yourself—
that is a girl who has lost something
significant.

Is it a man?
Is it her dog?
Her country?

You may have had the urge to offer me a map,
a Swiss army knife, or a spoon.
Because my eyes were bowls all empty
of soup and I was obviously
very hungry.

I could never really speak about it.
I just knew something was missing.
A phantom limb haunting
the tips of my fingers
the inside of my throat
tickling my mouth.

In the afternoons
I would go around searching
for impossible threads.

Something to ground me
to the earth, buckle me back in
to myself.

It was only when someone asked me
casually, hey, how's the poetry going?
that I realized what I had lost.

It's funny how that happens.
How the wilderness provides clues.
How another curious mind
can beckon my own lost mind.

How the tools are always there
just waiting for us
to pick them up
again and again.

True Kindness

If you push me
you will lose me.

If you waste my time
you will not receive it again.

True kindness is a woman who knows
the worth of her presence
my soul told me one day
when I was 38.

Work

The work now
is to keep the heart open, strong, and alive
no matter what happens.

This is hard work.
The tallest order.
The deepest prayer.

I wake in the morning
and clean my heart
like a window.

Some days
the storm lashes and
birds of peace break their wings
against the glass.

But I begin again
each day.

For this is good and honest work.
The only work
that matters now.

Brace Yourself

The year I fell in love with you
was the same year I learned
that nothing and no one belongs to me.

My instinct was to pull my heart back
safely into my own chest.

But I have never felt beautiful
wearing a gown
threaded with fear.

Never once felt safe keeping
a careful and whispered soul.

So instead
I release you
over and over again
so that my arms may trust the wisdom
of letting you go.

So that when you come back
each and every day
it is because you are full
and you are
free.

Untether

Let death remind you
just how useless it is
to live anyone else's life
except for your own.

Let the drum of your heart
carry up and over the incessant noise
of everyone else's agenda.

You did not come here
to be told what to do
but rather to unfold into
your own innate knowing.

Untether yourself from anyone
or anything
that makes you forget
who you are.

Our Love

When I think of you now
I think of your tenderness.

How you showed me
with the sound of your voice
and the movement of your body
how much you cared for me.

I think about how you didn't know yet
what it meant to be a man.
How no one ever showed you.

So instead you understood
how to be a person.
And when you met me
we met with force.

I recognized you.
Eye to eye.
One soul
appreciating
another.

Hi.

These are not small things.
These are memories
that make up a life.

The gentleness you gave me
shaped me.
The conversations we had
moved me.
The friendship we built
made me stronger.
And I carry that into my life
today.

And I remember
that day we took our love
to the edge of the cliff
and I asked, you first?

No, you.

Here, take my hand
and then let it go mid-air.
Feel the ferocious water
as we plunge
and then let us swim
our separate ways.
Sun and moon guiding us
as we go.

No matter where you are
my love will keep you,
your eyes told me.

And it has.

I hope that my love
has kept you too.

Resemblance

Years ago your mother woke very early.
She made you a sandwich, put it in a bag,
left her keys on the counter and walked—
cautiously beyond the yard at first,
into the street, down the block and further.

You stood there for many years after.
Never clutching anything.
No certain song inside your throat.
Only a silence that began and spread
throughout your chest, your limbs,
and your eyes.

In the evenings, in private, you allowed your hands
to smooth over her photograph, once or twice
dozens of times. Your fingerprints laid there
upon her face. The grooves of your skin
embedded.

It was a harmful thing.
All of that handling
with not very much at all
to hold.

You may not notice her now
if you saw her somewhere.

Your breasts the same size as hers.
Your mouth that particular shape.

You would perhaps look her over.
Lift your wrist from the table and let
your small shoulders fall but
no voice there with which to speak.

Nothing to mention
about common things
like lifting ornaments
from a box or bare legs
draped from a swing.

Face

Keeping up appearances
is so exhausting
that I never learned
how to do it.

This is my face.
I have freckles
and my mother's mouth.
My eyes are my dad's.
You will find in them
both passion and
sadness.

Here is my heart
my mind
and hands.

When you see me out
on the street
my face will greet you
with whatever I am working with
that day.

So feel free
to be whoever you are
as well.

It's ok to be quiet.
To just nod with love.
No words at all.

I don't have the time
or the skills required
to make things up.

And I just don't want to.

Courtship

Romance your poems.
Lay your papers in the sun.
Pour your body through them.
Put red lipstick on.

Ghosts

It never truly unthreads—
the fabric of a love that levels you.
After years of no sight
and I almost think
it's all gone.

I fall asleep
on an ordinary night
and there you are
clear as day.
Blushed cheeks, laughing.

Talking to me as if
we never, ever stopped.

Moving as if
I still know how
to handle you.

Morning comes and I am
10 years older
and the days of my mind
unfold all of the hours I've grown
without you.

All the homes I've lived in
between ours—

tending flowers
washing dishes
filling bathtubs
making love.

Who am I to say
that the long sleep of our conversation
has not been divine?

Who am I to say we didn't plan it this way
long before we knew how to speak?

Born

I have my own pair of ribs
here within
my small and mighty frame.

I've never borrowed them.
They have always been mine.

And I am more tempted by freedom
than I am by fruit.

It's Been Ten Days

I go from the bed to the window.
From the window to the door.
Because when the mind is haunted
the body still knows.

My skin has been
turning into air—
holding everything and
nothing.

Not my bones.
Not my blood.
Not my muscle.

Certainly not my
self.

The weight is still too much.

If I could stop this
I would.
If I could understand this
I would.

But the mind knows nothing
so I follow the body
light as it is
out to the porch

and into the sun
where there are
thousands of mornings
pressed into earth.

This comforts me.
This I can see.

I can make sense of the
sparrows and the sky.
The secret language
of trees.
The sound of leaves
touching each other's spines.

The way the dog howls
at the fence.
The shifting of
hours
wandering into
the moon.

This, my body knows.
So I lie down on the ground
and let nature remind me who I am.

My mother calls me from the kitchen.
She still has her mind
and so it is always working—
supper time

bath time
bed time.

None of that matters,
I whisper to myself.

Fasten yourself to the earth.
Remember who you are.

Let Your Wounding Be Your Blessing

Pain can deepen our awareness
of the fragility of life.

Seemingly breaking through
all of our resources
until we see that pain
is a resource.

A generous catalyst—
inviting us to forge a new path
and find a better way
to live.

Home

Run the water.
Pour the salt.
Fill the tub.
Lay your beautiful body way down.

You're a soft thing.
You're a fierce wing.
You're a million mornings
pressed into the sun.
You're a moon that rose
when the day was not yet done.

You deserve to rest.
To linger in water.
To pray and to ponder.
To adore your own skin.
To love the home you live in.

For Charlotte

My skin has no voice.
It lies here across my bones
thin as third-hand fabric
and the soul beneath it
calls and wanders, calls and wanders.

They believe I've lost the will to touch.
When once I traveled the entire length
of his collar bone to his knee
with the mouth of a plum ripening.
All that sensation—
now there is nothing.

No will, no fruit, no seed.
An empty mouth, open, unable to close
just yet.

And my eyes they are full
of sand, desert sand.

The kind of sand that fills an entire life and
never un-fills, but piles up and
makes strange homes inside my pores.
Sand castles without a sea.

No strong water to even me out.
No salt to mend and thread through

the ache, the longing
the rough, stand-off, solitary evening.

I may be old,
long gone, people never mind.
85 years full of limbs.
Skin falling away boldly.
A sacred battle in this body.

But I do remember
the sound of his bed.
Covers pulled back
and the beautiful body waiting for me there.
Purring, warm and inviting.
Ready for anything.

How my own body moved and
opened before
revving up.
A gentle and important work.

How I learned about my own life
through love
making.

It doesn't leave you, you know.
The will to
touch.

The love only grows.

And this is why I must leave the body
to feel that ease again.

Time

The soul will not settle
but it may wait a few centuries
for you not to.

The soul has time.
Sky time.
Depth of the ocean time.
Stars, entire galaxies kind of time.

You go out into the world.
Fall down and fall over
as many times as you need to.

The ten year detour, sure.
The career that was never yours, alright.
The love that took a whole life to get over, fine.

The soul gets it.
Your soul is the best friend
you ever had.
And the soul has all the time in the world
for you to return back
to your own self.
Whenever you are ready.

Because the soul will not settle.

In Touch

Hold people tightly and yet
lightly.

Give them room
to change.

When you meet again
in the afternoon or
evening somewhere
tilt your head so that
you ear is bare and open
and then ask—
How are you, my friend?
How have you changed?

This is what
lifelong relationships
are made of.

We are always dying
and so we must
re-introduce ourselves
again and again
to stay in touch.

Can It Be Beautiful?

The geometry of your arms
has changed.

They circle days and weeks and months
that I cannot understand.

My arms have changed too.

I sit here with my desk and my pens
waking every day to carry less and less
while you long to
carry more.

Your eyes see things
I do not see.

My hands move toward things
that do not matter to you.

Our lives have simply
and painfully
grown
apart.

But here is your beautiful heart.

And here is the day we met.
The friendship
we kept.

The hours
we spent
growing up and out
of our baby bones.

There isn't a word
for women
leaving a friendship.

There isn't a song
for the pain.

For every secret kept so sound.

But can the ending be beautiful?
Can we honor what we found?

Enough

Enough.
Enough water under the bridge.
I forgive you.
I forgive me.
I set us both free.

Within

She understood
that it all began
with her.

The responsibility
the possibility
and the love.

She found delight
and strength
in this
knowing that all she
really needed
came conveniently
from within.

The Never-ending Ending Of Things

No one is coming to rescue you.
No one is coming to make
the sea of your life
any less rough.

All storms and beauty and miles of water undone.

It is this way for each of us.
We all get swept away
tossed around
face in the sand
gasping for air.

Alive, almost gone, alive, alive, alive.

And then we see that breath
is a luxury of lungs
promised to no one.
And in that knowledge
we begin to float.
Turn our tender and once fearful face
to the sun.

Appreciate everyone.

I once harbored an anger.
It flowered so deeply inside of me

that you could see it growing wild
across my eyes.

Then the water came
to show me how I could not garden
this pain.
How nothing would ever grow.
So I headed to the ocean
and left it
in the bend of a wave.

We are here for such a brief time
and in the midst of it all
some days there is a surrendering.
A trust.

Bones of the body
finally relaxing into
the never-ending
ending of things.

Leaving

You were nautical and landlocked.
Your fins so hot and wild without water
in this world.
And so you had to let your body go.
I know, I know.

Hold On

What does the day bring?

So many sorrows stacked up
like hard-bound books
on an already unsteady case.

Nails falling out
all over this place.

The coffee brews quietly.
I skipped the morning
and soon it will be evening.

Strands of hair
still in my bed.

We must get through
the winter.
Pull on one sock
and then another.
That year the pandemic came
and then stayed.

The Light Behind Your Eyes

See this body I have been given?
My wrists, thighs, elbows, chest, and throat—
they were not made for you.

My legs were made to carry my mind
through many cities.
My arms were made to circle the people I love.
To carry the weight of books I can read
and groceries to bring home.

My throat it holds my voice and
the necklace my grandmother gave me.

May I, with the grace of all that is good and true
remember what my body is for.
May I pass this knowledge along
to every girl and woman I meet
so that she too can remember.

May we allow ourselves to forever flourish
among all the new soil
and with love
kick the old dirt
away.

It is the light behind your eyes and breasts
that matters.

Olive Tree

You are sleeping tonight
in the home I grew up in.
I know the creak in the hallway
the old window
the poetry I wrote
behind the clothes and in
the cupboards.

Roosters declaring morning relentlessly.
The goat determined and yelling.
Planes overhead
sheep chatting
wheels turning
flowers blooming forever
in a wild garden my mother made.

Sleep well there,
my love.
Wrestle with your dreams
and questions about
existence.
You are strong, safe, and blessed.
You are in exquisite company
with two of the most interesting people
I have ever met.

You will be
51 years old next week.
You sleep under the same roof tonight
as my mom and dad.
We think we get older
and it's true that we do.
But the ways that we soften and steady.
Learn how to truly be alone.
Have confidence in our own body.
Say goodnight and mean it.
Can we finally admit that
it is better this way?
Closer to death than birth, I mean.
It is ok to say so.
It is ok to not be young and to be very happy.
It is a comfort to know yourself so well
through years of living.

You fit into my family
in ways I never
could have imagined.

A steady presence.
An inquisitive hand.
A loving heart.

Picking olives
from the front yard tree
of my childhood home.

Sending me a photograph of
little buds
not yet ripe
while I sleep a state away
in a home we have made
together.

You were not born into this family,
lion love of mine
but you have made it
so sweet.

Plans

It happens
like you never thought it would.
Life, I mean.

You make a plan
and then God grins
and sways.

Take these days.
Live them
with as much courage
as you can.

They will not
come again.

Django

My mind mentions you, mentions cities.
Recalls mornings, afternoons, and
all of those evenings.

How I pressed myself up against
the inside porcelain of your old
clawfoot tub
while the light bulb above
flickered and dimmed.

How I lay there in the water
luxurious and calm as you danced
in the next room to Django Reinhardt
pausing to pour wine into modest mugs
that we re-used for our morning coffee.

We were hungry as orphans then.
Yet less obvious in the ways that we mourned.

And I remember how we slept,
very cautious at first of the space
and then how there was no space.
Our bodies gaining courage, gaining strength.
Until we woke up in the morning
unable to decipher one from the other.

How we preferred it that way.

Meanwhile, outside
the sparrow bowed his small head
upon electricity.

He was strong with the sound of planes
and steady with beginning.
Knew better how to navigate this love
than we did.

And as his feet lifted from the wire
I would perpetually wonder
if I put my mind away
would you migrate always
toward my thought.

And if I put my mouth away
would you seek the sound of my voice
when it left carried among
the urgency of trains and other things
that could not stay.

Out Of My Hands

So much time I have wasted
on chapters of my life
that were already written, read, and closed.

Thinking I could
change the dialogue
rewrite the scene
leave it better, sweeter, kinder.

Whole paragraphs
out of my hands.

Brave Flesh

When you lose someone you love
the shape of your world indents.
An arrow that becomes a part of the very skin
you were born in.
You wonder how you will live with this thing
protruding inward.

Surely everyone can see the puncture.
The giant, wailing crack
that began in your heart
split through your breast bone
upward toward your mouth
making your words uninhabitable
even to yourself.

How are you to describe on a common day
what it feels like to live with this?

Why even try?

You wonder how the sky still knows
how to hang high.
How the streets know how to unfurl
through cities and towns and states.
How the woman in her yard
with flowers and fruit

has hands steady enough to grow things.
How the chapel bell still rings.

You wonder how the wound will mend itself
because you don't have a thousand years
and surely that is the time it will take.

And yet you know
that no one is meant to live for very long
and that death will make a memory
of us all.

So you grieve
you beg
you bargain.
You beat the shit out of
your tennis shoes as your feet
pound the sidewalk.
March up canyons and hills.

You lie in the bath and you weep.
You stand at the stove and you must eat
because death is coming for you too.

But not yet
and not today.
So you summon
your own self
your fortitude
your ability to love

even when death
attempts to
bury your heart.

Even when loss lingers
at the doorstep of your mind
whispering—
It's all too much to lose.
It's all too much to lose

And it is.
IT IS ALL TOO MUCH TO LOSE.

So you fold the loss into
the corner of your heart
reserved for unbearable things
so that the rest of your heart can carry
your lifeblood into the days
you must still live and fight for.

You do this because
somehow you know you were born
to love and then to lose and then to love again.
You do this because your heart is made of
brave flesh.

The kind of beating that will bend and break
but mostly bow
over and over again
through each and every loss

and then pump blood deep into your chest
full of scars and sorrow and sweetness
declaring, I am alive. I am still here.

Howl

Come put your burdens down
just for a moment
and breathe in the ocean so vast.

Look at the lighthouse to the left
with your swollen and salty eyes.

Let it remind you
that your heart
is a tower.

Your soul
a prayer of light.

I know this
about you.

When you forget,
this old poodle dog and I
will howl your spirit back to you.

Even if it takes
all afternoon.

Even if it takes
our whole life long.

Relax

It is enough to make food.
It is enough to make songs.
It is enough to be a mother.
It is enough to be a dad.
It is enough to be an incredible friend.
It is enough to teach the alphabet.
It is enough to be a waitress.
It is enough to be a poet.
It is enough to be an explorer.
It is enough to be a dog walker.
It is enough to be nothing at all while you are figuring out
who you want to be.
It is enough to be an attentive listener.
It is enough to be a student.
It is enough to be an artist.
It is enough to be an inquisitive soul in a large world.
It is enough to be human.
Relax.

You are so much more than what you do.

Porcelain

I was still people pleasing then.
Pretending that my face was
porcelain.

Until one day
the cup of my mind
cracked wide open
and I remembered—

I answer first and
forever
to myself.

Can You Forgive Yourself?

Can you forgive yourself
for every time you were
a fool?

For the days you spent
running around
in the dark?

Can you take yourself
into your own arms
and give the beast in you
a warm bed
to sleep in?
A soft light to be
seen in?

Will you show the shame
the bright moon of
your face?

Give that trembling some grace?

Living is a mess
and you will make mistakes.
Can you grow better from them?
Can you not use them
to lash again and again
at your own heart and mind?

Can you be kind?

Mistakes are so much more useful this way.
Illuminating the path
you do not want to take.
Revealing the person
you do not want to be.

This is an abundant discovery.

Fallacy

Hear the siren roar
and the back buckle.
Feel us lose the thread.
The white knuckle.

Up against the wall
you clearly said—
It's you or it's me.

That is the deepest fallacy.

Same Side

When women cut
each other down
the sword is
so much sharper.

I can handle
the belligerent blade
of a man.

I have centuries of that battle
already in my blood.

But sister,
not you and
not us.

I will not war
with women.

This is the first thing
to know about me.

The Bounty And The Broken

I think it's safe to say
we are all heartbroken.

I can see it in your eyes.
Can you see it in mine?

I pull on my sweater.
I put on my shoes.
I have plans for the summer.
I have music and food.

It seems we learn to live with both—
the bounty and the broken.
Threading them deep
into our hearts.
Holding hope and love.
Fine lanterns in the dark.

Noble Work

She felt the pressure
the expectation
the weight.

But then she remembered
that her ambition cannot be
bullied out of its unfolding.

She whispered to herself
that she doesn't need to rush.
That understanding herself
is a gentle and noble work.

Carried out one day,
one breath, one deep longing
at a time.

Next Life

When we meet outside of this
troubled world
kiss me.

Tell me you knew
the ending would happen
just like that
and then laugh
and hold me
close.

Whisper your secret longing
for the next life.
Then unfurl the deep wings
of your dear heart
all sound, sweetness, and sky
and meet me there.

Moon

My body is changing.
I lie in bed
with other changing bodies.

My dog's arms have circled and buckled
tightly into her breast
and her eyes carry a blue fog
swept in over the years across her iris.

There is a man here as we sleep
and he is aging too.
His beautiful hands
thick with the day
and all he chooses to carry
toward the bounty of our lives.

I sleep by the window.
Breasts falling.
Body thickening.
I tend to take up most of the bed
and after all these years I am still
unabashed about that.

We have side tables with books.
We have our own lamps and dreams.
There is water should we need it.
There is a luxury of comforters and pillows.

When the dog stirs suddenly in the night
it's the man who wakes and worries.
He reaches for her small body, tenderly
and takes her out into the yard.

I wake only when they return
and reposition my body
to curl around my most beloved bodies.

While all along
there is a moon melting us
closer to the sky.
Illuminating our love.
Our deep, nourishing sleep.
Whispering, these are the moments
these are the nights
your heart will return to
again and again.

Begin Again

Little moments. Running the water. Tending to the plants. Cutting the fruit. Opening the curtains so that the entire sky can greet you. It's never easy but, no matter. Steam from the tea so quiet. An open book, and door, and arms.

You woke up today. You are alive. This is a gift. Even though life may beat you down. Hard. Even though things, situations, and people you love may be taken away from you so that your arms can memorize the grace of letting them go. Even then, especially then, begin again.

Remind yourself that nothing really dies; rather, it transforms. Everything and everyone you have ever loved lives in the mysterious memory of your cells. Turning, healing, renewing itself. Until one day, a photograph of someone very dear— long gone—visits your mind and you bow your head with appreciation.

Meanwhile, take your pain to the sea and your trouble to the mountain. Leave it there and walk home clean. When failure knocks and rattles and quakes, let it. Watch it make a fresh canvas of you. Failure, the great teacher, is kinder if you thank her as you are getting up off the floor. She knows something that you don't know—she is usually the last face you will see before breaking through. Such a little light in the crack of the door.

But today, if you are wading through the waters of loss or confusion, begin again. Open the avocado. Draw the bath. Gather the books. Play your favorite album. Write. Create art. Open your arms. Move your legs. Lovely, little blessings. Whispering to life that you won't give up.

Not ever.
Not ever.
Not ever.

Appreciation

Trev
Thank you for loving me for the poet creature I am. It's a passionate and nourishing life we keep. I love you.

My Family
I have been blessed with a family who understands me and also appreciates artists. I know what a gift this is. My family is composed of several beautiful individuals who I admire and love. I would like to especially acknowledge three people among this group: my brother, Matthew, my mother Anne, and my father Albert. We grew up together and much of who I am is because of who you are. Thank you for your love.

Lilly
Lilly, you were a three-pound poodle who changed my life in tender and miraculous ways. Your companionship is a gift I will always remember. Thanks for finding me. I needed you.

My Girlfriends
I am thankful for the beautiful friendships of my present, my past, and my future. My friendships with women have nurtured and fortified me ever since I was a little girl. It's a precious connection and there is so much to learn here. Thank you for traveling through the years with me, no matter how long our road has turned out to be.

My Readers

This book may have not been made without your sweet messages asking me for it. Thank you so much! I have loved hearing your stories, reading how a poem made you feel, and seeing the amazing ways you have taken one of my poems and turned it into another form of art. You inspire and encourage me. I am humbled by your love and appreciation.

Leonard Cohen

The fact that you were a person who lived gives me a lot of hope. Your music is always in the back of my mind and in my heart. Thank you for being such a thoughtful poet and songwriter, for taking your time with things, for showing me how it's done.

Orchid Street

I would like to thank the street I grew up on. Thank you for letting me come home. Thank you for being a flower. Thank you for Karen & Gary, Laura & Matt and their amazing daughters. Thank you for putting up with me while I grew up. Thank you for being a place I could receive mail. Thank you for being the foundation of the most formative years of my life.

About The Poet

Jeannette Encinias is a writer and teacher from California who spends much of her time on the Oregon Coast with her dog Oliver and her husband, Trev. Her poetry has been featured in books, plays, love letters, one-woman shows, and even an opera! She is a wildflower arranger, a strong coffee drinker, and her mother's daughter. Jeannette believes that words can change lives and sometimes even save them. Her own life has been saved by the poets and musicians that came before her and for this she is eternally grateful. To find out more about her work visit her website at www.jeannetteencinias.com

Ingram Content Group UK Ltd.
Milton Keynes UK
UKHW041437110423
419976UK00004B/342